FUNDRAI$ING
as a Career

What, Are You Crazy?

Linda Lysakowski, ACFRE

FUNDRAI$ING
as a Career

What, Are You Crazy?

Fundraising as a Career: What, Are You Crazy?
One of the In the Trenches™ series
Published by
CharityChannel Press, an imprint of CharityChannel LLC
30021 Tomas, Suite 300
Rancho Santa Margarita, CA 92688-2128 USA

www.charitychannel.com

In the Trenches, In the Trenches Logo, and Design are trademarks of CharityChannel Press, an imprint of CharityChannel LLC.

ISBN: 978-0-9841580-0-3
Library of Congress Control Number: 2010926388

13 12 11 10   8 7 6 5 4 3 2 1

Printed in the United States of America

This and most CharityChannel Press books are available at special quantity discounts for bulk purchases for sales promotions, premiums, fundraising, or educational use.

About the Author

Linda Lysakowski, ACFRE

Linda is President/CEO of CAPITAL VENTURE, a full service consulting firm with offices throughout the United States. Linda has managed capital campaigns ranging from $250,000 to over $30 million, helped dozens of nonprofit organizations achieve their development goals, and has trained more than 17,000 professionals in all aspects of development.

Linda is one of fewer than 100 professionals worldwide to hold the Advanced Certified Fund Raising Executive designation. She is a graduate of the Associaton of Fundraising Professionals (AFP) Faculty Training Academy and is a frequent presenter at regional and international conferences, including AFP conferences and CharityChannel Summits.

Linda is also a prolific writer; her books include: *Recruiting and Training Fundraising Volunteers*, *The Development Plan*, contributing author to *The Fundraising Feasibility Study—It's Not About the Money*, and co-author of *The Essential Nonprofit Fundraising Handbook*.

Acknowledgements

I would like to thank my publisher, CharityChannel Press and its CEO, Stephen Nill, whose guidance and friendship over the years have been invaluable to me. Also the many friends and colleagues I've met through the Association of Fundraising Professionals (AFP), whose inspiration, dedication and friendship have meant so much to me over the twenty plus years of my career. And my consulting clients whose daily work "in the trenches" is living proof that fundraising is indeed a profession of the noblest kind.

Linda Lysakowski, ACFRE
Las Vegas

Contents

Foreword

Nonprofit fundraising is actually more than a career. As you will learn from this book, the focus and goal of nonprofit work is not to build stockholder equity or produce a profit, but rather to implement the mission of the organization in a way that utilizes its resources, both human and financial, to the best benefit of the community(s) it serves.

Organizations in which nonprofit fundraising professionals work are typically corporations, albeit ones that are not profit motivated. However, as with any corporation, they are also businesses that require sound operational, ethical, and professional practices.

Nonprofit organizations that seek charitable contributions need to attract and engage donors who have an interest in the mission of the organization. Donors will want to fully understand and identify with the organization's case for support. Donors want and expect a good return on their charitable investments. The degree to which an organization is professional in the way it provides its programs, services and operations, often determines the extent to which they will attract donors, volunteers and employees. That is why the fundraising professional is so critical to the success of a nonprofit organization.

This book will help you appreciate the opportunities and challenges of the fundraising profession. There are some similarities between being a fundraiser and a salesperson: You need to believe in and know your product. It is important to qualify (do your research on) your customers (prospective donors), engage them in a conversation to learn about their needs and wants (passions), educate them about your product as it relates to their needs (case for support), close the sale (make the ask), and follow up with them after the sale (stewardship).

However, there are also many differences. Fundraising is all about relationships. Within this book are excellent examples of organizational indicators and personal characteristics that people interested in fundraising as a profession should consider before moving into a development position within a nonprofit organization.

Deciding on a career in development/fundraising is only part of the equation. Selecting the right organization that meets your interests and passions is just as important. In order to engage others and obtain their support for the organization for which you are employed as a fundraiser, you first have to sincerely believe in and support its mission and be able to celebrate the work of the organization. You can't ask others to believe in and commit their financial resources to an organization that you do not fully support yourself.

Becoming a successful fundraiser does not happen overnight. There is much to learn and experience before you can achieve full success. Take advantage of the suggestions Linda Lysakowski offers in this book. As with any successful endeavor, most of what contributes to that success is what takes place before the activity. Do your homework. Research and planning in advance of entering the profession of fundraising will be invaluable to the start of your career. Seek good role models and mentors along the way. Recognize that nonprofit work requires a significant personal and time commitment. Be willing to take risks and learn from your mistakes and the mistakes of others. Fundraising is like a roller coaster ride. There will be peaks and valleys, thrills and disappointments, surprises, rejection and success. You will need to be able to handle it all and stay focused and positive. As with so much in life, if you think positive, look positive and act positive, others will more likely want to join and support you. Not all fundraisers are winners. As described in this book, there are ways to learn how to be a winner, enjoy work, and achieve success as a professional fundraiser.

If you are as fortunate as I have been as a nonprofit executive, consultant and fundraiser, you will do so much more than raise significant funds for the organizations with which you will work. You will meet fascinating and very special people. These include co-workers, volunteers and especially donors who fund the programs and services that touch and benefit so many who would otherwise be without. You will experience the joy of enabling people to achieve their philanthropic goals and dreams. You will also experience pride associated with helping donors become role models for their families, their communities and especially for future generations.

In response to the question posed in the title of the book, "What, Are You Crazy?" I can answer from personal experience. No! A career in fundraising is not crazy. It could very well be the best decision you will ever make in your career development.

Norman Olshansky
President and CEO
Van Wezel Foundation
Sarasota, Florida

Introduction

As I was preparing to write this book, I came upon an article that so closely expressed my views of how fundraising is perceived by many outside of, and even within, the nonprofit community, that I wished I had written it myself. This article really struck me as one that relates the unfortunate state that fundraising is in for many nonprofit organizations. Boards and CEOs often do not recognize fundraising as a viable career and an important leadership position within their organizations. With permission of the author I am reprinting his article in its entirety:

Equal Rights for Fundraising
Dan Pallotta

Fundraising is the black sheep of the nonprofit sector. Charities spend as little as they possibly can on it. They talk as much as they possibly can about how little they spend on it. The watchdogs, the IRS, and donors deduct goody-two-shoes points from nonprofits in direct correlation to every dollar they spend on it. Institutional funders penalize charities for spending on it; it's a cannibal that eats program dollars. By extension, fundraisers are the black sheep of the sector's workforce; second-class citizens to the program staff who are in the trenches every day doing the real work of social change.

This is ass-backwards. Without fundraising there are no programs. The less we spend on it the less money there is for programs. Period. Spend more on it. Spend and spend and spend until the last dollar no longer produces a penny of value. This is how to maximize program dollars. George Overholser, founder of the Nonprofit Finance Fund, said to me that we should "decriminalize fundraising." I had never heard it put so accurately, either in terms of the way we treat it or what we should do about it. I would go a step further. We should make fundraising a program domain in and of itself — every bit as important as the medical research, social services, advocacy and everything else it makes possible. We should consider all spending on it to be critical "program" expense. Instead of disdaining it, we should invest in understanding and developing it, because unless we do, we'll never have anywhere near the money we need to address the massive social problems we confront.

Fundraising is the front line of civic engagement. Investment in fundraising is investment in understanding social behavior, generosity, altruism, the reasons people give and don't give, why they give to some causes and not others, and what would make them give more. To understand fundraising is to understand what inspires people and what doesn't. If we want to inspire people to change the world, we would do well to remember this.

I have long advocated for equal rights for charity with the rest of the economic world. Today I am advocating for equal rights for fundraising with the rest of the charitable world. When an AIDS researcher's experiment fails to discover a cure, her lab's expenses on the experiment are not moved to the "overhead" side of the books. Experimentation is a process of elimination. The data is considered crucial to the ongoing effort to understand how to cure AIDS. Why should fundraising be treated any differently? When a fundraiser's new event fails to bring in the amount of money she hoped for, valuable data is generated that will inform the future. It should not be treated as if it has no value. It is every bit as valuable as the AIDS data. Without it, there is no AIDS data.

Imagine telling an AIDS researcher that she cannot test any therapy unless it is sure to work. Yet this is exactly what we tell fundraisers; any idea you have that doesn't work will be characterized as a liability against our administration-to-program ratio and will hurt us, and, by extension, you. I was consulting with a major NGO about a new fundraising effort that could potentially raise millions. Its leadership would not go forward with it unless they could assure themselves in advance that it would net 65 cents on the dollar in the first year. Two years later, they still haven't made up their minds. If the fundraising effort itself were considered a program expense crucial to understanding what moves people with regard to this cause, they could report to the public that 100 percent of funds went to the cause, regardless of the results of the event; X percent to traditional program services and Y percent to study giving dynamics for the cause. It's a holistic approach. And it's far more authentic, accurate and honest than telling people that Y percent was wasted on overhead that contributed not one cent to the cause.

Fundraisers could experiment. Fundraisers could learn. The same way an AIDS researcher learns. Instead, we direct fundraisers to repeat the same methods over and over and over again, producing the same predictable and inadequate results. Is it any wonder that charitable giving has remained constant at about 2 percent of GDP ever since it's been measured?

Institutional funders should take the lead on this. Fundraising should be every bit as prevalent on the lists of their program interests as health, human rights, and global poverty. And when they are, they won't need to be giving program grants to health, human rights, or global poverty anymore; because the fundraising arms of the organizations they support will be able to fund them on their own.

It is our job, as fundraisers, to change this perception and I hope through this book to start this process.

Writing this book has been a real honor and privilege for me because it is dedicated to the thousands of people who work each day in the nonprofit sector to bring hope and healing, to educate and train, to invite the arts and culture into our lives, to protect the earth, and to advocate for those who cannot speak for themselves. I have been continually amazed at the profusion of nonprofits in the United States and beyond, and by the amount of time and money being contributed to support the many issues that these nonprofits are dedicated to promoting.

Fundraising has been around for more years than many people realize. Among the founders of the United States of America were those who could be considered some of this country's first professional fundraisers, including Benjamin Franklin. These founders worked tirelessly to raise money to build hospitals and schools in this new country that rivaled those of their European homelands. For many years, it was mostly the larger institutions of higher learning and health care that actually employed fundraisers. In recent years, however, this has all changed. Today, many nonprofit organizations employ at least one development professional and fundraising is becoming a respected career. Still, some people might feel that fundraising as a career is just one step above that of a used car salesperson. Or perhaps even one step below!

If you are one of those people, I hope through this book to change your opinion of fundraising as a profession and to inspire you to venture into the world of philanthropy. Or, if you are already part of this world, my wish is that this book will help you feel empowered and inspired by your work. It is my sincere desire that each day you will go to work eager to jump into the day with both feet, and with your head and your heart focused on enabling your organization to succeed in its fundraising goals.

In this book we will talk about the nonprofit sector and what it means to be employed in this sector. We will also discuss the many types of careers that are available in fundraising, so that you can find the right one for you!

You will find a chapter on the characteristics that make fundraisers successful. And we will talk about how you can actually acquire these characteristics for yourself. And, you will learn how to get started in your fundraising career.

In every fundraiser's career there comes a time when you will need to make some tough decisions—do I seek a promotion to a position of more responsibility? Do I use my fundraising career as a springboard to an executive position? Is it time to move on to another organization? In the final chapter of this book, I will offer some insights into making these decisions.

Certain key facts about fundraising and nonprofits will be highlighted in special sidebars, marked "Important!" And each chapter will end with a checklist of things for you to get started or advance in your fundraising career.

I encourage you to use this book as the first step in your new career and to continue to read, attend conferences, and network with your colleagues. Don't forget to continually educate yourself about the career of fundraising along with the technical aspects of development. I also invite you to email me and let me know the challenges and the triumphs of your own fundraising career (linda@cvfundraising.com). And, most of all, I wish you success in your fundraising career, no matter which of the paths in this book that you decide to follow.

What I Cover in this Book:

Chapter One: What Does it Mean to Work in the Nonprofit Sector?

This chapter will present an overview of the size and scope of the nonprofit sector. It further outlines the various types of nonprofits in which you might find a career in fundraising and lists the things that make working in the nonprofit sector different from working in the for-profit sector.

Chapter Two: Options in Fundraising Careers

This chapter includes the various different specialties that are available in fundraising and helps you determine if you have a propensity for being a generalist or a specialist. Hints on finding the appropriate size and type of organization for which you want to work are included in this chapter.

Chapter Three: Fundraising as a Profession—What Does it Take to Succeed?

Some of the qualities that make a great fundraiser are discussed in this chapter. It includes a discussion of everything from being a hard worker to having "presence." You will learn how to get started in your fundraising career or how to advance in your career if you are already a fundraiser.

Chapter Four: Making the Transition to Development

This chapter provides hints for you to make the transition into development, whether you are coming from another position within a nonprofit, from a career in the for-profit world, or from a volunteer role in a nonprofit.

Chapter Five: Starting on the Right Foot

In this chapter, you will learn the keys to getting started in a fundraising career without making a serious misstep. Key questions to be asked before accepting a position will provide insights into assuring success.

Chapter Six: Changing Paths in Fundraising/Moving On

Once you've been in a development position for several years, you will probably be thinking about advancing in the profession. This chapter provides insights into moving from a development position into an executive role or into a level of increasing responsibility. You will also learn when it is time to "shake the dust" and move on to another organization.

Appendices

The appendices include information that you should find useful, such as:

◆ Code of Ethical Principles and Standards of the Association of Fundraising Professionals (Appendix A)

◆ The Donor Bill of Rights (Appendix B)

◆ A report on salaries for charitable fundraisers (Appendix C)

◆ Reasons why donors give (Appendix D)

◆ Suggested Reading (Appendix E)

◆ My pick of the top 15 online resources for looking for a job as a professional fundraiser (Appendix F)

◆ Glossary of terms every professional fundraiser should know (Appendix G).

Sidebars

Throughout the book, I use sidebars to call attention to something that's particularly important, to give practical tips that you can use, and to define important terms that you, as a professional fundraiser, need to know.

There are some things that EVERY professional fundraiser should know. When you see an "Important" sidebar, it's important!

To help you succeed, I provide practical tips whenever they would help you to establish and succeed in your career as a professional fundraiser.

Every profession has its lingo, and fundraising is no exception. To smooth the way, I offer definitions that will have you sounding like a seasoned pro.

Chapter One

What Does it Mean to Work in the Nonprofit Sector?

IN THIS CHAPTER

- ···→ How large is the nonprofit sector?

- ···→ How many people are involved in the nonprofit sector?

- ···→ What makes the nonprofit sector different from other sectors?

- ···→ What types of organizations do fundraising?

- ···→ How do I get started in fundraising?

L et me tell you about how I entered the profession of fundraising; it might be a familiar story to some of you. Back in the 1970s, probably before some of you were even born, I was a banker. Most banks, partly because of the Community Reinvestment Act and partly because they wanted to be good corporate citizens, encouraged their employees to be active volunteers in their communities. Like many other bank employees, I eagerly volunteered for numerous fundraising activities including working on my alma mater's annual corporate appeal. This was the first time I realized that there was actually a profession of fundraising;

that people actually got paid to ask for money! Gee, I had been doing it as a volunteer for many years and loved the feeling of satisfaction that came with obtaining a commitment for a gift to the annual appeal, working on a successful fundraising event, talking to a group of business colleagues about the great work a nonprofit was doing in our community. Wow, I could actually get paid to do this???!!! How hard could this be if volunteers could do it?

Then one day I opened my file drawer at work to look for a file for a project I was working on for the bank and realized that there were more files in my drawer for my volunteer nonprofit activities than there were for work projects. Perhaps it was time for a career change! Before I knew it, I found myself as Assistant Vice President for Institutional Advancement at my alma mater. I quickly found out there was a lot more to fundraising than I had imagined. Not long after starting my new career I attended a CASE (Council for the Advancement and Support of Education) conference and had to quickly learn terms with which I was not familiar—LYBUNTS, SYBUNTS, fulfillment rates, nonprofit bulk rate indicia, planned giving, and many more. What had I gotten myself into?

One thing that immediately struck me, when I announced to friends and coworkers that I was leaving the bank to become a member of the nonprofit fundraising community, was their question, "Why would you leave a career in banking and take a pay cut?" (Actually I was getting a pretty healthy increase in my salary.) It helped me realize that most people tend to think nonprofit employees receive, and probably deserve, a much lower salary than other professionals. After all, they are working for a nonprofit—doesn't that mean that the organization is poor? Wrong!

For many people new to the whole concept of the nonprofit sector, there is a great deal of misunderstanding of what it means to be a nonprofit. Some think it means the organization can't operate in the black, because it then becomes a "for profit." Many people think that nonprofit staff should be paid less than standard wages because they are working for a "charity."

For clarification purposes, let's start with what it means to be a nonprofit organization. In the United States, a charitable nonprofit is usually a 501(c)(3) agency, a designation received from the Internal Revenue

Service after meeting certain requirements, most importantly that the organization serves a charitable, education, scientific, or community service purpose. Individuals can deduct donations to approved nonprofit organizations when filing their federal tax returns. Most government agencies and foundations will only make grants to nonprofit organizations.

Contrary to popular opinion, being a nonprofit does not mean that the organization must operate in the red or that it cannot have a fund surplus.

By receiving nonprofit status, these organizations are exempt from paying most federal and state taxes. Sometimes the nonprofit community is called the third sector (as opposed to government or the business sector), the independent sector, or the voluntary sector. There is even a new term being floated: the community benefit sector. All of these terms are appropriate and accurate. Most nonprofits are thought of as charities, although some are huge operations such as major universities and health care systems, but they still share the commonality of being a nonprofit entity since no individual or group of individuals benefit from the surplus revenues of the organization.

LYBUNTS—donors who gave Last Year But Unfortunately Not This.

SYBUNTS—donors who gave Some Years But Unfortunately Not This.

Fulfillment Rates—the number of pledges actually paid against pledges made. A 90 percent fulfillment rate is considered average.

Nonprofit Bulk Rate Indicia-the postage mark that is used by nonprofits entitled to post bulk mail at a lower rate than for-profit companies.

Planned Giving—often used to describe deferred giving such as a bequest or charitable trust.

So how big is this sector, and how many does it employ?

The following statistics from the National Center for Charitable Statistics might surprise many of you. As I write this, these are the most recent facts about the sector.

Nonprofit Organizations

◆ Currently, 1,514,821 tax-exempt organizations are registered with the IRS. This number includes 956,760 public charities and 112,959 private foundations. *(Source: The Urban Institute, National Center for Charitable Statistics, Business Master File 12/08.)*

> The main characteristic that separates a nonprofit from a profit-making entity is that no individual or group of individuals can benefit financially from the profits of the agency. This doesn't mean, though, that the agency can't make purchases, hire employees, or pay reasonable salaries. Whew! Aren't we glad to hear that!

important

◆ In addition, 443,464 other types of nonprofit organizations, such as chambers of commerce, fraternal organizations and civic leagues, are registered with the IRS. *(Source: The Urban Institute, National Center for Charitable Statistics, Business Master File 12/08.)*

◆ In 2006, nonprofits—including public charities, private foundations, and all others—accounted for 8.11 percent of the wages and salaries paid in the United States. *(Source: The Urban Institute, National Center for Charitable Statistics, Nonprofit Almanac 2008.)*

◆ In addition to these organizations, an estimated 377,640 religious congregations currently serve their communities in the United States. *(Source: American Church Lists.)*

Public Charity Finances

◆ In 2007, public charities reported over $1.4 trillion in total revenues and nearly $1.3 trillion in total expenses. *(Source: The Urban Institute, National Center for Charitable Statistics, Core Files 2007.)*

◆ Of the nearly $1.4 trillion in total revenues, 22 percent came from contributions, gifts and grants and 67 percent came from program service revenues, which include government fees and contracts. The remaining 11 percent came from "other" sources including dues, rental income, special event income, and gains or losses from goods sold. *(Source: The Urban Institute, National Center for Charitable Statistics, Core Files 2007.)*

◆ Public charities reported nearly $2.6 trillion in total assets in 2007. *(Source: The Urban Institute, National Center for Charitable Statistics, Core Files 2007.)*

Volunteering and Charitable Giving
One thing that makes the nonprofit sector different from other sectors is the fact that so many people actually volunteer not only their money, but their time, to help these organizations succeed.

◆ Approximately 26.4 percent of Americans over the age of sixteen volunteered through or for an organization between September 2007 and September 2008. This proportion has remained relatively constant since 2003 after a slight increase from 27.4 percent to 28.8 percent in 2003. (*Source: Current Population Survey, September 2008.*)

◆ Charitable contributions by individuals, foundations and corporations reached $314.07 billion in 2008, a decrease of 2.0 percent from 2007 after adjusting for inflation. *(Source: Giving USA 2009.)*

◆ Individuals gave $229.03 billion in 2008, a decrease of 0.1 percent from 2007 after adjusting for inflation. *(Source: Giving USA 2009.)*

◆ In 2008, religious organizations received the largest proportion of charitable contributions, with 35 percent of total estimated contributions going to these organizations. *(Source: Giving USA 2009.)*

◆ Educational institutions received the second largest percentage of charitable contributions, with 13 percent of total estimated contributions going to these organizations. *(Source: Giving USA 2009.)*

◆ Giving to grantmaking foundations, which accounted for 11 percent of total estimated contributions in 2008, received the third largest percentage of charitable contributions. *(Source:* Giving USA 2009.*)* Some further explanation about the *Giving USA* statistics:

◆ Individual giving, at $314.07 billion in 2008, includes estimated charitable deductions on tax returns filed in 2009 and an estimate of charitable giving by taxpayers who do not itemize deductions.

◆ The charitable bequest estimate of $22.66 billion reflects estimates for charitable deductions on estate tax returns filed in 2009 and giving by estates not filing federal estate tax returns.

◆ Individual giving and charitable bequests combined are estimated to be $251.94 billion (82 percent of the total).

◆ Foundation grantmaking reached an estimated $41.21 billion. Of that, about $18.5 billion is likely to be from family foundations, based on the percentage of family foundation grants in 2007 reported by the Foundation Center. Grantmaking by corporate foundations is in the estimate of corporate giving.

◆ Individual, bequest, and estimated family foundation giving combined are approximately $270 billion, or 88 percent of the total. Individual giving and family foundation giving added together are about $248 billion, which is approximately 81 percent of total giving.

◆ Corporate giving is estimated to be $14.50 billion. This includes estimated grants made by corporate foundations.

So what do all these statistics tell us? The nonprofit sector, and fundraising, is big business! The Association of Fundraising Professionals (AFP), the largest association of individual fundraisers in the world, has more than 31,000 members and there are many, many more people working in this field who are not members of AFP. While it is difficult to unearth statistics showing how many fundraising professionals there actually are, if just 20 percent of the public charities in the United States employ just one fundraising professional, that makes almost 200,000 professional fundraisers in the United States alone. And, of course, many of these charities are large ones that might have a development staff of dozens of people (universities, for example) and even mid-sized organizations often employ two to ten development staff persons. I would safely estimate, therefore, that there are close to a half million individuals in the United States that list their profession as fundraising, development, advancement, philanthropy or some term that involves the obtaining of funds for a charitable organization.

Who are these people and how do they find their paths leading to a career in fundraising? The professional fundraiser usually enters the field from one of these avenues:

◆ Another career in the nonprofit sector (social work, ministry, teaching, etc.)

◆ The for-profit sector (attorneys, bankers, business owners, etc.)

◆ Volunteers: an individual who has volunteered for an organization, such as a board member or committee member and subsequently moves into a paid fundraising position within that organization or another nonprofit.

To Recap:

The nonprofit sector is big business, with more than a million and a half nonprofits in the United States that account for more than 8 percent of all wages paid in this country. Revenues

MORE SPECIFIC TO FUNDRAISING, HERE ARE SOME STATISTICS FROM THE GIVING INSTITUTE'S PUBLICATION, *GIVING USA 2009*:

We estimate that American individuals, corporations, and foundations donated $307.65 billion to charitable causes in 2008. This is a drop of 2 percent in current dollars (-5.7 percent adjusted for inflation), compared to 2007. That is the biggest drop since Giving USA *began recording the data in the 1950s. Despite the decline, charitable contributions were an estimated 2.2 percent of Gross Domestic Product. Giving was 2.3 percent of GDP in 2007, when donations soared to an estimated $314.07 (current dollars) billion.*

important

of public charities totaled more than $1.4 trillion in 2007. Approximately 26.4 percent of Americans over the age of sixteen volunteered for nonprofits in 2008 and all of us are affected by the work of nonprofits.

In 2008 more than $307 billion was given to charities by individuals, corporations and foundations. Professional fundraisers are the people responsible for garnering this level of support. People enter the field of fundraising from a variety of careers. Some come from the for-profit world, some have been in other positions within a nonprofit and some begin as volunteers and then move into professional fundraising.

No matter what career path led you to the world of philanthropy, you might find that fundraising can be an exciting and challenging career. However, as with any career, you might also find that it is not as easy as many people think it is!

PRACTICAL TIPS TO GET YOU STARTED IN A FUNDRAISING CAREER:
• Learn about the nonprofit organizations in your community—how many are there, which ones do you admire the most, which ones do other people speak highly about, do they have a development staff, how do they raise money?
• Choose three to seven organizations for which you might want to work and research them. Which ones are financially stable, transparent, adhere to their missions and have a value system that is consistent with your own value system?
• Meet with the executive directors of these organizations and the development staff if there is one. Find out about their long-term goals and any possible plans for hiring development staff.

practical tip

Chapter Two

Options in Fundraising Careers

IN THIS CHAPTER

···➔ What types of positions are there in fundraising?

···➔ Would I rather be a big fish in a little pond or a little fish in a big pond?

···➔ Do I want to be a generalist and "do it all?"

···➔ Would I rather specialize in one aspect of fundraising and, if so, what types of specialties are available?

So, once you've made the decision that "fundraising is for me!" what types of options are available to you?

You will have to start by making a few decisions. Some questions you should ask yourself might include: "Would I like working for a large organization or a smaller one? For what type of organization would I like to work? Would I like being a generalist, or a specialist?"

The first decision should be what type of organization you would want to work for. What are your interests? Children? Animals? The arts? Education? The environment? Other? It is essential that you work for an organization about whose mission you are passionate. There will be many options within your area of interest once that is determined. For someone with varied interests the field is even broader. For example, if you love reading, a library is an option, but perhaps you also love the outdoors, so that opens another realm of possibilities in recreation areas or environmental agencies. If you are also an animal lover you could look at various animal rescue groups or shelters. A music lover? You could look for a position with a symphony or a music festival, but you might also enjoy the arts in general so a position in a museum or a dance company might be another option for you. If social justice is your hot button, you could seek a position in an activist or advocacy agency or an organization that deals directly with an issue such as fair housing or feeding the hungry.

Another decision that must be made, although this decision might change during your career in fundraising, is whether working for a large organization or a smaller one is more appealing to you. Some advantages of working with a larger organization include:

◆ It might have a more stable financial position and a larger budget for fundraising.

◆ It might be better known in the community.

◆ There is usually more access to support staff.

◆ Better benefits such as educational opportunities and health care might be available.

◆ There is generally a larger development staff and, therefore, the opportunity to specialize.

◆ There will be more opportunities for advancement.

◆ A national or international organization might offer opportunity for travel.

On the other hand a smaller organization often offers:

◆ Access to top management and board members whose involvement in fundraising is critical.

◆ The ability to make quick decisions.

◆ The chance to be a generalist and encounter more variety in your daily work.

◆ An opportunity to grow the development program

◆ More flexibility in your work schedule.

◆ The opportunity for more autonomy.

You need to make your own decisions about the things that are most important to you—salary, benefits, flexibility, opportunities for advancement, the chance to be autonomous, travel opportunities, etc. You should strive to make your career move based on these criteria. As mentioned before, these criteria might change during your career and this change in priorities often leads to a change in position or organization. The lack of advancement opportunities is one reason why there is such a high turnover in this field—estimates are the average development officer stays in one position for less than two years.

Generalist or Specialist?

Once you have decided what type of organization you want to work for, the question is which is more attractive to you—being a generalist or a specialist? One of the advantages of working in a small organization is that for those who enjoy being a generalist, the one-person development office offers an opportunity to learn about all the aspects of development, from Internet fundraising to planned giving and capital campaigns. Many people thrive on that type of atmosphere; they really enjoy doing a little bit of everything. And it is a great way to learn about the various types of careers in fundraising that might develop into a desire to specialize in one of these aspects. Also, running a one-person shop often is a good training ground for moving into a position of supervising a staff of development people or even preparing for a career as an executive director or a consultant.

So, what are some typical specialties one finds in the development office?

Planned Giving:
This is a career path often chosen by attorneys, financial planners or bankers who want to leave the for-profit world and work in development. While not usually as high paying as a career in law or the financial world, it is generally one of the highest-paid positions in the profession of fundraising. Many of these professionals find that, although there is a significant cut in salary compared to the typical earning level of attorneys and financial planners, they enjoy the nonprofit world because of a passion for the mission or just because they want to leave the corporate world behind them. Many attorneys and bankers who have left the corporate world report that they are much happier in the nonprofit community where they feel they are really making a difference.

> Major Gifts are generally defined as a gift at a level that requires special treatment, such as personal solicitation, special recognition, etc. Major gifts levels are defined differently by each organization. In a university or large nonprofit, a major gift could be $100,000 or even $1 million, and in some smaller organizations, a major gift might be $500 or even $100.
>
>  **finition**

Major Gifts:
Most organizations value individuals who have had experience in obtaining major gifts and have a track record of success. If you enjoy meeting face-to-face with individual donors, you might opt to specialize in major gifts. Financial planners, attorneys and bankers often find this career path attractive, particularly if they have dealt with high-income clients in a former career. This is a highly-sought-after specialty that generally comes only after years in the field. However, many development professionals in entry level positions strive to learn as much as possible about major gifts fundraising so they can specialize in this area.

Campaign Specialist/Director/Manager:
Some people really enjoy the fast-paced world of capital campaigns and, in a large organization such as a university where campaigns are usually

ongoing occurrences, there might be openings for people who work exclusively on capital campaigns and special projects. Once you develop experience in capital campaigns for one organization, you can easily move into becoming a capital campaign specialist in a larger organization where campaigns are prevalent, or even into a consulting career.

Annual Giving:

Many individuals enjoy the annual giving part of fundraising. While some might think that it is boring and repetitious, the annual giving program is the key to developing major donors. Positions in this area might involve managing the direct mail program, a telephone program and Internet fundraising in a smaller organization, or managing just one of these components in a larger organization. An "annual fund generalist" who works in all aspects of the annual fund might find that one area is particularly appealing and might decide to focus even more narrowly on direct mail, for example. Positions with a very narrow focus like this will generally only be available in very large organizations.

Corporate Giving:

Many individuals, particularly those who came into the fundraising profession from the corporate world, will find corporate giving challenging and rewarding. This area of fundraising might include drafting proposals for corporate foundations or organizing an annual business appeal. If you come from a corporate background, your contacts can prove very valuable to the nonprofit organization seeking corporate support. As a business person entering the fundraising profession, your experience in the business world might be very attractive to an organization that is trying to increase the level of its corporate fundraising efforts.

Special Events:

Some people just love throwing parties, and although there is a lot more involved in running special events than being present at the event itself, including seeking sponsorships, managing the calendar, preparing the budget, recruiting and working with volunteers, special events might appeal to you. If you have volunteered at the organization's special events, you might be interested in working as a staff person coordinating events. Because special events can be so labor intensive and draining, staff members who start in this position often seek to move into more integrated fundraising roles where they have an opportunity to work on various fundraising projects in addition to events.

Writing:

If your passion is the written word, there are positions in development for grant proposal writers and those who can write a good case for support, as well as other fundraising materials developed from the case. Journalism majors or people who have worked in the media often look for a career writing for nonprofits. Many larger organizations offer this specialty. In smaller organizations, the development officers might do all the writing themselves or might outsource some of this to an outside contractor.

Research:

If you enjoy doing research and working with data, there are opportunities to research individuals, corporations and foundations. Those with technical skills, good logic and persistence might find this an ideal development position. Universities and other large organizations generally have a department of researchers. In smaller organizations this task usually falls under the chief development officer's duties or might be outsourced.

Data Entry/Donor Management:

If you are skilled at managing data, you might find this position rewarding. Managing a donor database is one of the key positions in any development office, so a good database manager will be a highly-sought-after individual. This

---

SOME PRACTICAL TIPS TO HELP YOU FIND YOUR NICHE:

• Take a personality test and find out if you are a person who sees the big picture or if you really like to get into the details.

• Talk to people in the development profession and ask them what they like and don't like about their jobs, what their biggest challenges are, and what their greatest rewards are.

• Volunteer at a large organization to help in its development office and get a flavor for all that it takes to run a large development program.

practical tip

position includes preparing development office reports and sometimes research as well as stewardship of donor records. Individuals interested in technology and the Internet, and who have great organization skills, might be well suited for this position.

Titles

Position titles will vary from organization to organization and there might be variations of any or all of the above positions. But in a larger development office, there is generally a Chief Development Officer, Vice President, or Director of Development who manages the rest of the staff. In a small office, the Director of Development will likely be responsible for all of these tasks.

The chart illustrates the development functions and how they might be distributed in an organization.

One Possible Development Office Chart

To Recap:

There are many decisions that you must make when considering a career in fundraising.

First, what type of organization do you want to work for? Options include arts and culture; animal rights groups; advocacy groups (for many causes); education (from preschool to universities); religious or faith-based groups, including churches; human services; the environment or international organizations.

You also need to decide if you want to work for a large organization or a smaller one, after determining the pros and cons of each and considering your personality traits. Within larger organizations especially, there is the option to specialize in areas such as planned giving, capital campaigns, grant proposal writing, special events and other areas.

Some of us like to be a big fish in a small pond; others like to be a small fish in a big pond. Which are you?

Chapter Three

Fundraising as a Profession—What Does it Take to Succeed?

IN THIS CHAPTER

···→ What are the key characteristics of a successful fundraiser?

···→ Are these characteristics inborn or can they be acquired?

···→ What can I do as a fundraising professional to acquire or strengthen these characteristics within myself?

···→ What do I look for when hiring development staff people?

M any individuals entering the profession for the first time and those hiring their first development staff person are often not certain if they have "the right stuff" or what qualities to look for in a development professional. Often one hears that development is really just sales or marketing. The individual or organization about to embark into the world of development needs to understand that it is a profession in its own right. Being a good sales person or a good marketer might be helpful in fundraising, but there is far more to the career than sales and marketing. In his book *Born to Raise*, Jerold Panas lists the top ten qualities of a successful fundraiser as:

1. Impeccable integrity
2. Good listener
3. Ability to motivate
4. Hard worker
5. Concern for people
6. High expectations
7. Love the work
8. High energy
9. Perseverance
10. Presence

This is a tall order. What if you feel you do not have these qualities? Can they be learned? If so, how can you learn to cultivate them? Let's look at each one and see if there are things that can be done to cultivate what might seem, at first glance, like innate qualities.

Impeccable Integrity

Although professional integrity seems to be a quality that one either has or hasn't, there are things you can do to help develop your personal integrity. First know, understand, and support the AFP Code of Ethical Principles and Standards (Appendix A). This document will provide guidelines about what is ethical in the field of fundraising. Adherence to the Donor Bill of Rights (Appendix B) is another step in assuring that the organization holds the donor's interests above its own, and that you, the professional, hold the interests of the donor first, the organization second, and yourself last.

If you have a faith system, it can be a help in developing your sense of morality and ethics. Every major religious institution holds certain moral principles that can help its members make sound ethical judgments.

You can also enroll in a class in ethics and attend AFP programs on ethics. AFP also has an ethics board that can answer questions about ethical issues. So although integrity might seem to be an inborn quality, it can be developed by understanding ethics, morals and donors' rights. One thing that can help you develop professional integrity is to follow the hierarchy of judging whether a specific action, including the acceptance of a major gift, values the donor's interest above your interest, and even above the interest of the organization for which you work.

Chart: Hierarchy of Integrity

Good Listener

Good listening is definitely a quality that can be learned. A class in communications can help emphasize that listening is the most important part of good communication skills. (I personally think there is a very good reason why human beings were created with one mouth and two ears!)

Active listening is important to good donor relations. Often a major gift can be secured by a solicitor whose listening skills have been honed. Listening for what the donor's interests are is even more important than being able to persuasively explain the organization's case. Practice making "the ask" and truly listening to the donor through role playing with colleagues or by attending courses in making the ask.

Ability to Motivate

The ability to motivate donors, volunteers and staff is a critical key for success. Motivating donors goes back to the integrity section. Putting the donor's interest first and foremost will make it easier for you to motivate donors. Motivating donors does not mean persuading donors to do something that they don't want to do or that is not in their best interest. Motivating donors comes through understanding that philanthropy brings joy to the donor and that if the donor really believes in the mission, motivation is simply a tool to bring about the donor's wishes. Learning the case for support and having passion for the mission of the organization for which one works is the best way to successfully motivate another person to share that passion.

STAFF MEETINGS:
Regular staff meetings that include an educational segment about some facet of fundraising and occasionally a motivational or inspirational guest speaker, in addition to staff updates on current projects, can help motivate your staff to greatness.

It is also important for you to understand the psychology of philanthropy. (See list in Appendix D.) There are many motivating factors that prompt an individual to contribute to a nonprofit organization. Each donor will have different motivating factors that influence a decision to give or not give. Listening to the donor is a critical skill that can help you understand how to motivate donors.

Volunteers, likewise, can be motivated only if the volunteers and the fundraising staff share a passion for the mission of the organization. Again, a good course in communication will help you learn how to speak and write with enthusiasm and passion that will motivate others.

Motivating the staff of the organization is also important. This starts with having respect and concern for other staff members. Staff members will be motivated by the good example set by the chief development officer. Involving staff members in the development planning process is a good way to motivate them to help implement the plan.

Hard Worker

One thing you need to understand going into this profession is that it is definitely not a nine-to-five job. Often you might be on the job as early as seven a.m. meeting with volunteers, attending breakfast meetings or just getting into the office early to organize your day before the phone calls and emails start arriving. You might easily be at work at seven or nine p.m. attending after-hours events, meeting with volunteers, or working at a phonathon. The key is to work hard, but take good care of yourself at the same time. Eating healthy, getting regular exercise, having a hobby or interests outside of work, and taking a vacation or several mini vacations each year will keep you mentally and physically healthy even though the hours of your job might be demanding.

And, working hard does not mean you need to be "wired in" 24/7. Leave work at work. Do not take it home or on vacation unless it is extremely critical. In some cases, it might be better to answer emails while on vacation rather

PRACTICAL TIPS TO HELP YOU MOVE INTO OR GROW IN THE PROFESSION OF FUNDRAISING:

• Get to know development professionals and those in nonprofit leadership positions. Make a list of the ones you admire most and list the reasons why you think this person is a top professional in the field.

• Develop a long-term plan for your career, listing goals you want to accomplish before you retire and developing benchmarks to measure your own growth as well as the growth of the development program you are leading.

• Learn as much as you can about the development profession; develop a plan to attend at least one educational program each quarter.

practical tip

fhan becoming stressed out by the sheer volume of email waiting at the office on your first day back at work. But as a true professional be careful to avoid thinking that you are indispensible and that you have to stay connected to the office at all times. You aren't and you don't!

Concern for People

Again, this might seem like an innate quality that one either has or hasn't, but there are some things you can do to cultivate concern for people. First, working for an organization about which you care deeply is one way that you can feel concern for the organization's clients. Many professionals gravitate to an organization that might have helped them or a loved one and these individuals will usually be empathetic with the organization's clients. Another tool that can help is to get out and about within the organization, the old "management by walking around" theory. Talk to the people who use the organization's services, find out their stories and talk to them about their hopes and desires for the future. It will make fundraising easier and allow you to speak in a compelling fashion about your organization's mission and can also help you build empathy and concern.

Concern for people goes beyond caring about the donors and the clients, but extends as well into concern for the staff. Taking time to listen to the concerns of other staff people, your colleagues in the development office and others in the organization can help the development professional build a concern for people.

High Expectations

As a development professional, you should have high expectations not only for yourself, but for your organization and for your co-workers. Often it is the development professional that "leads from the middle" and inspires the organization to greatness. Cultivating donors who have vision is one way to lead the organization to a higher level of performance. Also, some board members can have a great effect on the vision of the organization, so as a development professional you should have input into the selection of new board members who can help transform the organization into bigger and better things. However, this does not mean setting unrealistic goals or having expectations that are so demanding that the staff gets frustrated.

Expecting the best from the development staff and other staff within the organization is critical as well. Development professionals who have a staff reporting to them should allow the staff members to set their own goals and provide them with the tools to do their job. Having a once-a-year staff retreat for the development office members in addition to regular staff meetings can be a good way to empower staff.

Love the Work
Not only do you need to love the organization you work for, you need to love the work of development! Loving this career often starts with volunteering in the area of development. If you do not enjoy volunteer fundraising, you probably won't love it as a career. So if you are thinking about entering the profession, you might want to begin by volunteering to work on a special event, a phonathon, or a corporate appeal for a few nonprofits and see if you really do love fundraising.

As with anything the more knowledgeable you become in an area, the more likely it is you will enjoy doing it. Who can say they love knitting if they don't know how to knit, or cooking if they have never learned how to cook, or skiing if they haven't taken a ski lesson? The same is true with development. You will need to learn as much as you can about the profession by taking classes, reading books, attending workshops. If you find a particular aspect of fundraising that really appeals to you, such as planned giving, major gifts, or grant writing you should pursue that area. If you prefer being a generalist you should look for a position as a development director in a small shop where you will get to do a variety of fundraising tasks. Finding your niche is critical to loving the work. It also means that if you become frustrated, worn out, or just bored, you might need to think about moving on.

High Energy

Having high energy seems like a natural for some people, whereas for others, it might require some work. But energy can be built by following some of the advice mentioned earlier. Eating right, exercising and relieving stress by taking time off can help boost your energy.

Using artificial stimulants like caffeine does not really give you a high energy level and might, in fact, cause the opposite when the temporary effects of caffeine wear off. A good herbal tea that relaxes might actually do more to boost your energy. Getting enough sleep at night also helps raise your energy levels during the day. Simple things like having nice artwork or a scented candle or oil in your office, or taking time off work to get a pedicure, can help build energy.

Loving the work will also help you have the high energy needed to work long hours; motivate donors, volunteers and staff; and meet the expectations you have set for yourself, or others have set for you.

LONG-TERM GOALS CAN HELP
Working on long-term goals for a specific amount of time each day can help. And understanding that you should focus 90 to 95 percent of your time on the 5 to 10 percent of donors who account for 90 to 95 percent of all the gifts your organization will receive helps as well.

important

Perseverance

One thing that senior development professionals have learned is that perseverance is a highly needed quality. Major and planned gifts, in particular, require building long-term relationships; perseverance pays off. If donors think the organization has forgotten about them they might just move on to the next organization.

If the development office needs to undergo a computer conversion, perseverance is definitely going to be required! This is a tedious and frustrating process and one that never seems to be completed in the expected timeframe.

So how do you cultivate perseverance? Part of the secret to perseverance is setting goals and realistic benchmarks to measure success. This will keep you from wanting to throw in the towel when the going gets tough. Strategic planning is one way to develop reasonable timelines for yourself, and help you understand that often good things take time. CEOs and development officers are often under a great deal of pressure to raise money quickly. Entrepreneurial board members who are shrewd business people are often accustomed to working on the basis of instant decisions, and might want the development office to just "go out and do it" without adequate planning. Be careful not to get so caught up in keeping your head above water that you do not have the time to plan. A recent survey asking development professionals what their biggest challenge is shows lack of time for planning as the leading challenge listed.

Of course sometimes your organization itself needs to cultivate patience and persistence, so helping to build a philanthropic culture within the organization is a big part of your role. In the next chapter, there is a quick and easy assessment to help determine your organization's commitment to building a philanthropic culture. One of your major tasks might be helping your board and executive staff understand that fundraising is all about building relationships and that if you persevere in this relationship building, your organization will benefit tremendously. If you can impart this knowledge to your organization's leaders, you will rise to the top of your field. You must take the time to plan strategically; otherwise your organization will be left behind in the dynamic and ever-evolving world of the nonprofit sector. Leadership should look at the return on investment of careful, strategic planning.

Presence

Presence might be the hardest to define and the hardest to cultivate in a development professional. Perhaps the closest thing to this might be a "perception of poise." A more contemporary definition might be closer to "positioning yourself." Presence can also be described as the ability to command attention and being respected as a professional.

So what can you do to develop a sense of presence?

First, look and act professional at all times. Development professionals, especially when meeting with donors or potential donors (which might be all of the time) should wear a suit and tie, or for women, a suit, nice dress or pant suit. Although some nonprofits adopt a more casual atmosphere, dressing for success is important for the development professional because you will be very visible in the community. And of course, you never know when that million-dollar donor might walk in the front door! Being well dressed and well groomed will give you a sense of pride and confidence that is necessary for a sense of presence. This does not necessarily mean that you need to spend a lot of money on clothes and a new car, but looking good and driving a respectable looking car can help add a sense of presence. Good posture and an open and welcoming facial expression can be very meaningful, especially when you remember that you only have one opportunity to make a first impression!

Of course, presence is about much more than just looking good. Knowing the job will make you appear more confident and knowledgeable, adding to the presence factor. So, not to belabor the point, education and training are critical. Read, attend workshops, and join a professional organization such as AFP!

To Recap:

There are several key traits that successful fundraisers have in common. These traits include impeccable integrity; being a good listener; the ability to motivate staff, volunteers and donors; being a hard worker; a true concern for people; having high expectations for yourself, your organization and other people including staff, volunteers and donors; perseverance; and presence. While some of these might seem to be innate qualities, there are things you can do to develop these qualities.

Success is measured in many ways—financial success, personal growth, happiness and a feeling of doing a job well, making a difference. How do you measure success?

Chapter Four

Making the Transition to Development

IN THIS CHAPTER

···➔ What are some of the things that might cause "culture shock" when I move into a development position?

···➔ What can I do to make the transition into fundraising easier?

···➔ What are some of the pleasant surprises I might find when entering a career in fundraising?

You probably did not grow up thinking "I want to be a professional fundraiser." As mentioned earlier, some of the paths professional fundraisers have typically followed include:

◆ Moving from another position within a nonprofit to a development position.

◆ Moving from the corporate world into a development position.

◆ Moving from a volunteer fundraising role into a development position.

Each of these transitions has its own unique set of challenges.

Let's talk about each of these pathways into the profession and the challenges that might be part of them.

Moving from Another Nonprofit Position

Many fundraising professionals have come from within the organization. Perhaps they were social workers, teachers, public relations staff, marketing staff, or administrative staff. Sometimes an executive director of one organization might move into a development position in a larger organization. Often clergy people, who have developed an affinity with the fundraising role of their vocation, move into full-time development positions. There are many more examples of the types of positions, from CEOs to clerical support staff, which have been a path into the development/fundraising field.

What are some of the challenges of this move? One thing that quickly becomes clear to the "newbie" to fundraising is that the role of the development staff is usually the least understood in the organization. Program staff, by contrast, fills a role that is pretty apparent in most organizations; there must be teachers in a school, counselors in a drug addiction facility, physicians and nurses in a hospital, etc. The symphony cannot perform without musicians and a conductor, a museum needs curators and educators, marine biologists are needed to run an ocean research center.

But fundraising/development—what on earth is that and why does the organization need someone to manage the process of fundraising? The role of development within the organization needs to be made clear to everyone in the organization. Successful organizations have visionary leadership. One way to convince leadership of the importance of development is by having them interact with the key nonprofit leaders in their communities. A CEO or board chair from a highly respected and successful nonprofit can often convince a struggling CEO of the value of having a strong development program.

Leaders want their opinions to matter, but might feel that development is not their area of expertise. They might want to spend their time on organizational planning, with which they are generally more comfortable. You, as a development officer, need to help your organization's leadership reach a comfort level with development and philanthropy and convince them that their insight is critical to the success of the development program.

Another drawback of moving to the development position from within an organization is that you might get sucked back into your previous role in the organization. It is easy for staff members to call on the person with the most experience in an area when they need help, so as a new development officer you might find yourself getting called on to help out your former department. People within the organization might also resent your promotion or might not accept development as a viable need of the organization, thinking that your talents might be better used in the program area. This is one of the reasons we need to, as Pallotta says, "decriminalize" fundraising.

On the plus side of making this move, you already know the organization and its mission, which means that it will be easy for you to develop a strong case for support and to market the organization. You might also be familiar with some of the organization's major donors and supporters, as well as its volunteers. And of course, transitioning into development from within the organization means that you already know the staff and possibly the board so there might be no need to spend a lot of time getting to know personalities and organizational culture. This learning curve can be quite intense for someone coming from outside the organization.

Moving from the Corporate World to the Development Profession
Many individuals enter the development profession after being part of the corporate world. Bankers, attorneys, financial planners, realtors, sales people and media professionals often gravitate to the nonprofit world after some exposure to this sector through their clients or colleagues. So what are some of the things you might face upon entering the development profession?

The first, and not among the least, is culture shock. If you are a business executive, it might be difficult to move into a field where often the hours are different, and the work ethic and the work climate are far different from that to which you are accustomed. Many nonprofits start their work day later in the morning but might work into evening hours. Development, of course, is not a nine-to-five job, but many corporate leaders are amazed at what they perceive to be a much more laid back approach to work that some nonprofits tend to have. You might be accustomed to a more competitive environment, where collaborations with agencies that might even be considered competitors are not something you have had to deal with before.

You also might never have dealt with the budget constraints that nonprofits often deal with on a daily basis. Particularly if a position is grant funded, it might disappear simply because the funding is no longer available. If you are entering development from a government position, this concept might be especially difficult to deal with. Nonprofits, unlike government agencies, cannot impose taxes when they need increased revenue. They must go out and raise the money. And unlike businesses, the program side of the organization is usually not expected to be profitable so there needs to be other sources of revenue generation.

While most businesses are ethical, the level of ethics and transparency required in the nonprofit sector might be new to many business people. If you are entering the nonprofit sector for the first time, you might be surprised at the fact that the organization's annual federal tax return, the IRS Form 990, is required to be available to the public and that because a nonprofit is basically a public trust it is required to be accountable to its donors and the public.

On the positive side, as a corporate leader you can bring much to the nonprofit sector. Every nonprofit can benefit by applying sound business principles to its operation. Some of the valuable skills business people, especially entrepreneurs, bring to the nonprofit sector are the ability to develop budgets, planning skills, meeting-management skills, and the ability to lead others within the organization. The corporate leader often brings valuable business contacts to the nonprofit organization—contacts

Assessing Your Organization's Philanthropic Profile

• Does your organization have a development office?

• Do experienced professionals staff the development office?

• Does your development budget include money for professional development (membership in professional organizations, conferences and workshops, books and periodicals, etc.) for the development staff?

• Has your organization allocated a budget for a donor software system to manage fundraising activities?

• Do your organization's staff members understand the importance of the development function? Do staff members support the development office's efforts?

• Does your organization seek to hire development professionals that are certified (CFRE or ACFRE, FAHP, GPC, etc.) or assist current staff in obtaining credentials?

• Does the chief development officer attend board meetings?

• Is your board committed to development (do board members give and get money for the organization)?

• Is there a development committee on your board?

• Does a development officer staff this committee?

• Is there clerical support for your chief development officer?

• Does your development staff act and look professional?

• Is your development office in a prominent location and does it have a professional appearance?

• Does your organization support the AFP Donor Bill of Rights?

• Is your organization aware of and supportive of the AFP Code of Ethical Principles and Standards?

• Does your organization understand the importance of donor-centered fundraising?

• Does your organization understand that it takes time to establish a development program, and that building relationships with donors is the key role of the development office?

• Is your organization committed to work with consultants when it is appropriate to do so, and not expect staff to manage major efforts such as a capital campaign?

• Is your CEO involved in fundraising?

• Are there volunteers involved in your fundraising program?

practical tip

that can be potential funders, sources of volunteers, or spokespeople for the nonprofit. And, often the successful business person might have innovative ideas for nonprofits in the area of profit-making subsidiaries or projects that can help the organization diversify its revenue streams without jeopardizing its tax-exempt status.

SOME PRACTICAL TIPS TO HELP YOU BECOME SUCCESSFUL AT FUNDRAISING:
• Make a conscious decision to work only for organizations whose mission you feel passionate about. Remember the adage—"do what you love and the money will follow."
• Strive to be a change agent within the organization for which you work. Develop a plan to educate the organization's leadership about philanthropy.
• Remember that the donor's interest is always the foremost consideration in any decisions involving fundraising.

practical tip

Moving from Volunteering to a Development Position

Many individuals have found their way into development through volunteering at a nonprofit organization. Volunteers who have worked at special events, volunteered for an organization's annual appeal, served on a development committee, or have been a board member might find that fundraising is really their niche and decide that they would like to work in the development area.

One of the drawbacks of taking this route is that often volunteers only see one side of fundraising. A successful event, an annual appeal that meets its goal, working as a team to develop a plan, or helping set development goals might not allow the volunteer to grasp the depth of a full development program. As a volunteer, you also might only see the surface of what really goes into a development program. You might not know how many hours a typical development officer works, how much detail-oriented work is involved in doing research or preparing development reports for the board. You might not understand that while a special event is deemed financially successful, the staff and volunteer hours that went into this event might not be the best use of human or other resources.

On the positive side, if you have been a volunteer, you are already familiar with the organization and obviously committed to its mission. You might also be familiar with the staff and the organization culture. Also, you will be able to identify with volunteers and will have a good understanding of how to identify, recruit and work with volunteers. Volunteers can often bring skills from another profession into the development office.

Understanding philanthropy and donor psychology is an important prerequisite for the profession of fundraising. In Appendix D is a list of reasons that motivate people to contribute to charitable organizations. Knowing and understanding that donors are motivated by many different reasons for giving will be essential to your success as a fundraiser.

To Recap:
Fundraising is one of the top ten growing careers, and fundraisers have moved from being thought of as just a tad higher than a snake oil salesperson to a member of a respected profession. People are moving into this career from several different avenues—the for-profit world, other positions within the nonprofit world, and volunteering. No matter which path has led you to seek a career in fundraising, there are adjustments that you will need to make when entering this career.

Fundraisers are often the least understood profession within a nonprofit. The hours are long and the expectations are high. You can make this transition easier by understanding the culture of nonprofits, learning as much about the profession as possible and by talking to other professionals as well as learning to build trust and confidence within your organization.

Chapter Five

Starting on the Right Foot

IN THIS CHAPTER

- ⋯➔ Ethics in fundraising—what do I need to know?
- ⋯➔ What should I look for when applying for a job in development?
- ⋯➔ What are realistic expectations of a fundraising professional?
- ⋯➔ How do I avoid being set up for failure?

No matter how you enter the career of fundraising, there are certain things you need to succeed. Among these are: a commitment to ethics and professionalism, the support of the organization for which you work so you can advance professionally, and a network of colleagues in the development profession to provide support.

Ethics and Professionalism
Ethics is critical, especially in today's environment of scrutiny, transparency and watch dogging. Whether you are a member of the AFP or not, you should be aware of the Code of Ethical Principles and Standards developed by AFP, and to which every AFP member must subscribe. These standards provide guidance in ethical dilemmas that might face the development professional. For AFP members, there is

also an Ethics Board that is available to assist in ethical decision making and to whom offenses can be reported, which might result in censure or even removal of membership for an AFP member who violates the code. A copy of the AFP Code of Ethical Principles and Standards is included in Appendix A. Other professional organizations, such as AHP (Association for Healthcare Philanthropy), have their own codes of ethics as well. (The AFP Code of Ethics is included in this book, not because it is the only code for fundraisers that is available, but because many of the others relate to a specific type of organization such as health care, or to a specific fundraising position, such as a researcher, while the AFP code is more generic.)

Another document with which you should become familiar is the Donor Bill of Rights. Developed by several leading professional associations, this document leads the way in building solid donor relationships based on the commitment of the development officer and the nonprofit organization to keep the donor's rights at the forefront of any charitable transaction. This document is included in Appendix B. I recommend that you post this Bill of Rights in your office and on your organization's website, and include it in printed material such as the annual report, newsletters and any publications that might be distributed to donors and potential donors.

Knowing that the organization and the development staff are aware of, committed to and active in promoting the Donor Bill of Rights and other ethical standards puts donors at ease and makes them feel secure in the knowledge that they are working with an organization that truly cares about its donors. One of the roles you as a development officer can take is helping the organization for which you work develop its own code of ethics. The development professional often takes a lead role in educating the board and staff of the organization in the ethical ramifications of fundraising.

Organizational Support
Another critical element to your success as a fundraising professional is having the support of the organization for which you work. Some

important questions that you should ask before accepting a position in any organization are:

◆ To whom does the chief development officer report?

◆ Will you have access to the board?

◆ Is there support staff available in the development office?

◆ Is there a development office budget?

◆ Is money allocated in the budget for professional development?

◆ Is there donor software in place, or is money budgeted to buy software?

◆ Is money allocated in the budget for other tools you will need, such as publications, research software, and dues and memberships?

All of these items are things you need in order to succeed. Unfortunately, organizations often decide to hire a development officer and have not thought about what tools this person will need to succeed.

Far too frequently, boards and executive directors, when considering bringing a development person on board, ask, "How long will it be before this person is raising more than the person's salary?" Nowhere else in a nonprofit is this question asked. Program people, by contrast, are usually not expected to "show a profit" by bringing in program fees that exceed their salary. Nor is the CFO asked to cut expenses that total more than the CFO's salary. But, for some reason, as Dan Pallotta notes, fundraising has somehow been the black sheep of the nonprofit world. This needs to change. You will need to have the full support of the organizations for which you work in order to be successful at raising money. Boards and management need to understand that development/fundraising is all about building relationships (that's why it's called development) and not just about the money! The money will follow once the relationships are solidified.

TITLES, TITLES EVERYWHERE!

There are many titles given to development staff people— Vice President of Philanthropy, Vice President of Institutional Advancement, Director of Development, and many more. For the purposes of simplicity in this book, I am referring to the person in charge of fundraising as the Chief Development Officer.

To Whom Does the Chief Development Officer Report?

If you are hired as the chief development officer, it is important that you report directly to the executive director or CEO of the organization and that you are part of the management team. You need to have input into developing the organization budget and should be responsible for the development office budget. The other administrators of the organization need to know what the development office does and how it supports the entire organization. "No money, no mission." You need to be part of the strategic planning process and any major decisions that might affect the organization's ability to raise funds from public and private sectors. Here is an organizational chart showing where the development office typically fits into the overall organizational structure.

One Possible Organization-Wide Chart

Will You Have Access to the Board?

It is also important that you have access to the board of directors. You should attend board meetings, support the development committee chair when the chair presents the development committee report and be available to answer questions about the report. You should also have access to work with individual board members to identify, cultivate and solicit major donors for the organization. The development person often is responsible for the education of the board in matters relating to fundraising ethics, theory and methodology. You should be invited to work with the board governance committee to evaluate individual board members and the board as a whole in their fundraising role and you should be invited to propose potential new board members who will be supportive of the organization's development program.

Is There Support Staff Available?

One disturbing trend in the hiring of development staff are organizations advertising for high-level development persons with many years experience in major gifts, planned giving and capital campaigns, and who also "must be proficient in Raiser's Edge" or some other software program. This is disturbing because if you are expected to spend all your time sitting at a computer managing donor data, you will not be out there building relationships that are so critical to success.

You should expect the organization to have a high-level clerical person

An interesting study done by the Foundation for California Community Colleges showed that a development staff of five or more provides greater efficiency and results, with an even greater efficiency at higher staffing and budget levels. This study cites that the larger development office (seven or more staff) typically raise $1 million a year per staff member, while smaller ones (two or fewer staff persons) raise less than $200,000 per staff member. In order to allow for maximum growth of the development program, the organization must provide the support needed by the development staff.

or development assistant that can serve as the donor database manager. In larger organizations, there are usually several staff persons to fill special functions, such as planned giving, major gifts, events, etc., but development staff should not be assigned to carry out functions that are not development-related. When applying for a development position, you need to know what other duties might be expected of you which could prevent you from doing the necessary development work.

Is There a Development Office Budget?
Of course, salary is usually the big question that development officers ask when applying for a position. However, there is more than just the salary to consider. Benefits might actually be better in a nonprofit than in many corporate positions, especially vacation and paid sick leave. While many persons think that nonprofit people are underpaid, there is actually a significant trend for fundraisers to be earning more as the profession matures. In Appendix C there is a report for AFP's salary survey that shows positive trends in salaries. AFP members can download the full report at the AFP website.

However, the organization needs to commit more than the cost of salaries and benefits for the fundraising staff person(s). There should be a departmental budget that will provide the support you need to be professional, efficient, and successful. For example, is there a professional-looking office with privacy for the development staff?

If you are relegated to a shared office, a spare walk-in closet, or an unprofessional-looking office, donors and volunteers will not feel comfortable enough to share their questions, plans and desires (and perhaps not even their money) with you. The development office also needs up-to-date equipment. Anything that involves communication with donors—a personal email address listing the organization's name, a cell phone with email capability, GPS system, etc. —are valuable tools that can help you be more efficient and productive.

Is Money in the Budget for Professional Development?
Another important thing to ask about the budget is whether there is adequate money for your continuing professional development.

The organization should pay for your membership in professional associations relevant to fundraising. Conferences, workshops and seminars are also important for you to keep up with the latest trends, educate yourself in areas of development in which you might not be proficient, and networking with other development professionals.

Is There Donor Software in Place, or Is Money Budgeted To Buy Software?

Often development professionals are expected to work wonders with very few resources. One critical resource for the development office is a good donor software package. You cannot be expected to build strong donor relationships if you do not even know the history of a donor's relationship with the organization. A good question to ask before accepting a development position is whether there is an adequate donor software system and how accurate the records are that are contained in this system. Has the donor information been kept up to date? Is there someone who manages the data? Is there a budget for training if the database manager needs additional training and support?

As mentioned earlier, as a candidate for a high-level development position, you should certainly be knowledgeable about donor software systems so you will know how to access the information and develop the reports needed to implement a strong development plan. But you should not be expected to actually enter the data and manage it.

Is Money in the Budget for Other Tools Needed By the Development Office, Such As Publications, Research Software, and Dues and Memberships?

The fundraising area is usually the least understood department in any nonprofit. Many people within the nonprofit community, including sometimes the CEO of organizations, do not understand the science and the art of fundraising. While the relationship-building part of your job is certainly an art, there are many tools that can make the science of fundraising more effective. Some of these tools include prospect research software or the ability to engage outside help to research potential donors, and books and periodicals that provide insights into both the art and science of fundraising. Membership in local community organizations such as the local Chamber of Commerce can enhance your ability to make contacts with potential donors and volunteers. All of these things should be included in your development office budget.

Building Professional Networks
Professional networks are essential to success. Another question you should ask before accepting a position is the level of support that the organization will provide for you to join and become active in an association such as the AFP. An organization that is willing to invest in its staff at all levels should be willing to pay for membership in AFP or a similar organization, and allow the development staff time during the work week for active participation in these organizations. You will grow tremendously in your development position if you are involved in leadership roles within a professional organization. The support of your employer in this area will help you advance in your career.

In addition to professional organizations such as AFP, most states in the U.S. have a statewide association of nonprofits that often have a focus on fundraising and development and can provide you with another network of professionals that can help support your career.

And of course, there are numerous online resources for building your network of development professionals. Social media marketing such as Facebook, Twitter, and LinkedIn can help expand your network and serve as a source of information or sometimes just provide a sympathetic ear to listen to your frustrations. The largest online community of nonprofit professionals is CharityChannel (www.charitychannel.com), which provides not only a huge professional network, but educational opportunities such as webinars, books and interviews with top nonprofit thought leaders.

Mentoring
One of the advantages of belonging to a professional association is the ability to get involved in a formal mentoring program. Many AFP

chapters offer programs that can be very formal ones, including group educational sessions and expected outcomes; others offer a more informal mentoring relationship based on the needs of the mentees. Whether formal or informal, a mentoring relationship is a great opportunity for "newbies" to the profession to learn from a long-time professional and/or one that offers expertise in a particular area, such as planned giving, from which the mentee can benefit greatly.

A mentor should be sought out either from within a professional association or through your personal network. Mentors can enhance your skills, boost your morale, and provide career guidance. Once you've been in this field for a while, you should consider serving as a mentor to other "newbies."

Personal Growth

One of the best ways to enhance your personal growth in the development profession is to look at the certification process. Fundraisers who have been in the field for five years or longer might be eligible to become a CFRE (Certified Fund Raising Executive). This certification has become a respected designation in the field and many job opportunities might

PRACTICAL TIPS TO HELP YOU BECOME A GREAT FUNDRAISER:

• Find a mentor early on in your career, either through a formal network such as AFP, or through your informal network of professionals.

• Look into the certification program available at your level of experience and start building your portfolio of educational credits, achievements, and service to your community and the profession so the certification and recertification process will be easier to manage.

• Once you've achieved a level of professionalism where you are thought of as an experienced, knowledgeable professional, be sure to share your expertise—teach classes, write for the profession, become a mentor to those new to the profession, and continue to expand your horizons, challenging yourself to ever greater things.

require certification or, at the very least, the job posting will state, "CFRE preferred." For more information on the certification process, check out CFRE International at www.cfre.org.

If you have been in the field more than 10 years and are already a CFRE, you might want to consider advanced certification. The Advanced Certified Fund Raising Executive (ACFRE) is a highly respected designation currently held by fewer than 100 professionals worldwide. Although the process is rigorous, it is rewarding both personally and financially for many individuals. To find out more about this process, contact AFP at www.afpnet.org.

To Recap:

Ethics and professionalism are critical in the field of fundraising. Public scrutiny of charities is on the rise. You will want to become familiar with the AFP Code of Ethical Principles and Standards and help your organization adopt its own code of ethics.

Organizational support is also crucial to success in this field. You will want to ask about this before accepting a development position. Find out to whom you will report, what staff support is available, and if the organization is willing and capable of supporting your professional development.

Greatness in fundraising, as in anything worthwhile, comes only with hard work, commitment and passion.

Chapter Six

Changing Paths in Fundraising/Moving On

IN THIS CHAPTER

- ···→ How can you advance to a leadership role in development?

- ···→ Can a career in development provide a path to an executive position in a nonprofit?

- ···→ How do I get noticed and considered for a promotion in the development office?

- ···→ How do I know when it is time to move on to another organization?

At some point in the career of every development professional there comes the time when some tough decisions must be made. Is it time to ask for a higher-level position within the organization? Do you "stick it out" in a position that has reached its potential, or is it time to "shake the dust" from your feet and move on?

In a larger organization there will be more room for growth into positions of increasing responsibility and visibility. In smaller organizations there is often not much room for growth unless you can move into a management position.

Moving into Different Development Positions
Often when you start in an entry level position in a development office, there is room for growth. For example, if you start as a development assistant learning the database and all aspects of fundraising, you might move into a position of more responsibility and eventually become the chief development officer. Some ways to prepare for this growth are to learn as much about the development office operations as possible. Learning the donor's interests and preferences can be helpful when you have the opportunity to move into the position of working directly with these donors. Learning valuable skills such as planning and working with volunteers can also prove helpful if you want to move into a new position in development.

One of the drawbacks of being promoted from within is that it is often hard for the organization's leadership to envision you in a higher-level position. Some ways to overcome this are to accept leadership roles whenever possible, to act and dress professionally and to display an air of confidence that comes with knowledge. Attending classes and workshops is helpful. Enrolling in a graduate program might prove to be a valuable move.

If there is a particular specialty in which you are interested such as special events, planned giving, or grants and foundation relations, learn as much as you can about that specialty to became the office's "expert" in that area. This could lead to a promotion or even to a new position being created within an organization.

Moving into an Executive Position
Once you reach the highest level within the development office, the options within that organization are usually limited to becoming an executive director. While this was not the usual path of development in years past, the likelihood of a development professional becoming the chief executive officer within a nonprofit is becoming more and more commonplace. In higher education settings, for example, more college and university presidents are coming from the development field than from the academic field. An experienced development officer will often have acquired the skills to lead an organization forward as its

chief executive officer. Skills learned in the development field such as planning, building strong relationships, and being the public "face" of an organization are easily translated into leadership positions.

Because good fundraising skills are valued in an executive director, organizations are more interested in promoting development professionals into leadership roles than ever before.

Moving to Another Organization
Sometimes, however, the only answer is moving to another organization. The wise development officer will see the signs well in advance so he or she can begin preparing for a move before it comes down to being let go by the organization, making it harder to find a new position.

Sometimes you wake up in the morning and just do not want to go to work! It happens to everyone. If it is just that it has been a bad day or a bad week, these thoughts usually disappear and you are ready to jump back in. However, if every day is starting to become a drag, then it might be time to move on. Often it is because organizational leadership has changed, perhaps a new executive director is on board and just does not understand fundraising or value the work of the development office. Perhaps a new chair has assumed leadership of the board and does not share the previous board chair's commitment to fundraising as a part of the organization's culture. Or a personality clash has developed between you and others within the organization. Sometimes these things can be worked out. But an executive director that does not value your input

SOME SIGNS THAT IT MIGHT BE TIME TO MOVE ON ARE:

•The executive director no longer values input from the development officer;
•The relationship between the board and the development officer is strained or nonexistent;
•There is lack of commitment on the part of the organization to developing a philanthropic culture;
•Expectations for the development officer are unrealistic.

practical tip

and decisions, is constantly overriding your decisions, or embarrasses you in front of staff, board, volunteers or even donors is a situation that no development officer should tolerate for an extended period of time.

Occasionally the chief executive officer feels threatened and cuts you off from relating with the board, volunteers, or even donors. Sometimes this can be worked out with intercession, perhaps from a board member or an impartial mediator. But if the CEO does not allow you a maximum amount of autonomy to build strong donor relationships, you might be doomed to failure.

If the organization refuses to budget adequately for development and sets unrealistic expectations of the development office, you will very quickly become exhausted and frustrated trying to meet these unrealistic expectations. This is why it is so important to focus on both monetary and non-monetary goals for the development office, and for management and development staff to develop expectations together and agree on measurement standards for success. Allowing enough time for a new development office to become mature enough to perform at acceptable standards is critical.

If you have decided that it is time to move on, go back to those networks that you've established. Seek guidance from a mentor. Learn or hone the appropriate skills that will help you in a new position. Maintain a positive attitude.

Many development officers find that after a period of time within the field, they have the desire and ability to move into a consulting position. This step should be carefully considered before "hanging out one's shingle." Consulting is hard work and many development professionals, while they love the work of development and are very good at it, might find the aspects of managing a business, marketing themselves and maintaining a healthy client balance far more demanding than working within an organization. While consulting offers you the freedom to work with a variety of clients and set your own hours, it might not be the choice for you. If you are considering consulting, you should talk to other consultants about the pros and cons before making this major decision.

You should also evaluate the marketplace to determine if there is a need for the services you want to offer and then develop a business plan. You also need to consider the benefits available within an organization and determine if you are ready to assume the costs of health care, a retirement fund and other fringe benefits that will not be available to you when starting out on your own.

In conclusion, the options are many, the organizations are myriad, the profession is growing, and the rewards are numerous. So, is fundraising as a career still as crazy as it might seem at first glance, or are you ready to jump in? Or if you are already in the profession are you ready to, as the poker players, say, "go all in?"

To Recap:

"When you reach a fork in road, take it." Yogi Berra

There will come a time in your career when we reach that fork in the road—should you seek a promotion within your organization, or should you think about moving on to a new organization or maybe even into a different career altogether? If you love the organization for which you are working, you might want to stick it out and try to be a change agent.

However, if you have lost all faith in the leadership of this organization or no longer feel you have credibility in the

PRACTICAL TIPS TO HELP YOU STAY WITH YOUR CHOSEN PATH OR CHOOSE THE PATH LESS TRAVELED:

- Take time to get away from your work occasionally and really get to know yourself and what makes you happy.
- Investigate all the paths open to the fundraising professionals, talk to consultants and leaders in the field about how they made their decisions about which path to follow and what they might do differently if they had to do it over again.
- Read more about the topic in some of the suggested reading listed in the appendix.
- Remember that the definition of philanthropy is love of humankind, and if you really understand the world of philanthropy, you will see fundraising as a means to an end and not the end itself.

 practical tip

organization, it might be time to "shake the dust" and move on. Having a mentor and/or colleagues you can rely on for support will help you make the right decision for you.

Appendix A

Code of Ethical Principles and Standards

ETHICAL PRINCIPLES Adopted 1964; amended Sept. 2007

The Association of Fundraising Professionals (AFP) exists to foster the development and growth of fundraising professionals and the profession, to promote high ethical behavior in the fundraising profession and to preserve and enhance philanthropy and volunteerism.

Members of AFP are motivated by an inner drive to improve the quality of life through the causes they serve. They serve the ideal of philanthropy, are committed to the preservation and enhancement of volunteerism; and hold stewardship of these concepts as the overriding direction of their professional life. They recognize their responsibility to ensure that needed resources are vigorously and ethically sought and that the intent of the donor is honestly fulfilled.

To these ends, AFP members, both individual and business, embrace certain values that they strive to uphold in performing their responsibilities for generating philanthropic support. AFP business members strive to promote and protect the work and mission of their client organizations.

AFP members both individual and business aspire to:

- practice their profession with integrity, honesty, truthfulness and adherence to the absolute obligation to safeguard the public trust

- act according to the highest goals and visions of their organizations, professions, clients and consciences

- put philanthropic mission above personal gain

- inspire others through their own sense of dedication and high purpose

- improve their professional knowledge and skills, so that their performance will better serve others

- demonstrate concern for the interests and well-being of individuals affected by their actions

- value the privacy, freedom of choice and interests of all those affected by their actions

- foster cultural diversity and pluralistic values and treat all people with dignity and respect

- affirm, through personal giving, a commitment to philanthropy and its role in society

- adhere to the spirit as well as the letter of all applicable laws and regulations

- advocate within their organizations adherence to all applicable laws and regulations

- avoid even the appearance of any criminal offense or professional misconduct

• bring credit to the fundraising profession by their public demeanor

• encourage colleagues to embrace and practice these ethical principles and standards

• be aware of the codes of ethics promulgated by other professional organizations that serve philanthropy

ETHICAL STANDARDS

Furthermore, while striving to act according to the above values, AFP members, both individual and business, agree to abide (and to ensure, to the best of their ability, that all members of their staff abide) by the AFP standards. Violation of the standards might subject the member to disciplinary sanctions, including expulsion, as provided in the AFP Ethics Enforcement Procedures.

Member Obligations

1. Members shall not engage in activities that harm the members' organizations, clients or profession.

2. Members shall not engage in activities that conflict with their fiduciary, ethical and legal obligations to their organizations, clients or profession.

3. Members shall effectively disclose all potential and actual conflicts of interest; such disclosure does not preclude or imply ethical impropriety.

4. Members shall not exploit any relationship with a donor, prospect, volunteer, client or employee for the benefit of the members or the members' organizations.

5. Members shall comply with all applicable local, state, provincial and federal civil and criminal laws.

6. Members recognize their individual boundaries of competence and are forthcoming and truthful about their professional experience and qualifications and will represent their achievements accurately and without exaggeration.

7. Members shall present and supply products and/or services honestly and without misrepresentation and will clearly identify the details of those products, such as availability of the products and/or services and other factors that may affect the suitability of the products and/or services for donors, clients or nonprofit organizations.

8. Members shall establish the nature and purpose of any contractual relationship at the outset and will be responsive and available to organizations and their employing organizations before, during and after any sale of materials and/or services. Members will comply with all fair and reasonable obligations created by the contract.

9. Members shall refrain from knowingly infringing the intellectual property rights of other parties at all times. Members shall address and rectify any inadvertent infringement that may occur.

10. Members shall protect the confidentiality of all privileged information relating to the provider/client relationships.

11. Members shall refrain from any activity designed to disparage competitors untruthfully.

Solicitation and Use of Philanthropic Funds

12. Members shall take care to ensure that all solicitation and communication materials are accurate and correctly reflect their organizations' mission and use of solicited funds.

13. Members shall take care to ensure that donors receive informed, accurate and ethical advice about the value and tax implications of contributions.

14. Members shall take care to ensure that contributions are used in accordance with donors' intentions.

15. Members shall take care to ensure proper stewardship of all revenue sources, including timely reports on the use and management of such funds.

16. Members shall obtain explicit consent by donors before altering the conditions of financial transactions.

Presentation of Information

17. Members shall not disclose privileged or confidential information to unauthorized parties.

18. Members shall adhere to the principle that all donor and prospect information created by, or on behalf of, an organization or a client is the property of that organization or client and shall not be transferred or utilized except on behalf of that organization or client.

19. Members shall give donors and clients the opportunity to have their names removed from lists that are sold to, rented to or exchanged with other organizations.

20. Members shall, when stating fundraising results, use accurate and consistent accounting methods that conform to the appropriate guidelines adopted by the American Institute of Certified Public Accountants (AICPA)* for the type of organization involved. (* In countries outside of the United States, comparable authority should be utilized.)

Compensation and Contracts

21. Members shall not accept compensation or enter into a contract that is based on a percentage of contributions; nor shall members accept finder's fees or contingent fees. Business members must refrain from receiving compensation from third parties derived

from products or services for a client without disclosing that third-party compensation to the client (for example, volume rebates from vendors to business members).

22. Members may accept performance-based compensation, such as bonuses, provided such bonuses are in accord with prevailing practices within the members' own organizations and are not based on a percentage of contributions.

23. Members shall neither offer nor accept payments or special considerations for the purpose of influencing the selection of products or services.

24. Members shall not pay finder's fees, commissions or percentage compensation based on contributions, and shall take care to discourage their organizations from making such payments.

25. Any member receiving funds on behalf of a donor or client must meet the legal requirements for the disbursement of those funds. Any interest or income earned on the funds should be fully disclosed.

Appendix B

Donor Bill of Rights

Philanthropy is based on voluntary action for the common good. It is a tradition of giving and sharing that is primary to the quality of life. To assure that philanthropy merits the respect and trust of the general public, and that donors and prospective donors can have full confidence in the nonprofit organizations and causes they are asked to support, we declare that all donors have these rights:

I. To be informed of the organization's mission, the way the organization intends to use donated resources and of its capacity to use donations effectively for their intended purposes.

II. To be informed of the identity of those serving on the organization's governing board, and to expect the board to exercise prudent judgment in its stewardship responsibilities.

III. To have access to the organization's most recent financial statements.

IV. To be assured their gifts will be used for the purposes for which they were given.

V. To receive appropriate acknowledgment and recognition.

VI. To be assured that information about their donations is handled with respect and with confidentiality to the extent provided by law.

VII. To expect all relationships with individuals representing organization of interest to the donor will be professional in nature.

VIII. To be informed whether those seeking donations are volunteers, employees of the organization or hired solicitors.

IX. To have the opportunity for their names to be deleted from mailing lists that an organization may intend to share.

X. To feel free to ask questions when making a donation and to receive prompt, truthful and forthright answers.

Developed by American Association of Fundraising Counsel (AAFRC), Association of Fundraising Professionals (AFP), Association for Healthcare Philanthropy (AHP), and Council of Advancement and Support of Education (CASE).

Endorsed by: Independent Sector, National Catholic Development Council (NCDC), Partnership for Philanthropic Planning (PPP), National Council for Resource Development (NCRD) and United Way of America.

Appendix C

Charitable Fundraising Salaries Increase Across North America

Source: AFP International (May 12, 2008)

Salaries for charitable fundraisers in the United States and Canada increased from 2006 to 2007, according to the latest Association of Fundraising Professionals' (AFP) Compensation and Benefits Study.

The average salary for U.S. respondents to the 2008 survey increased to $72,683 in 2007—a 2 percent increase from the average in 2006. Average salaries for Canadian fundraisers increased from C$71,827 in 2006 to C$74,376 in 2007—a 4 percent increase.

Location and type of organization play an important part in determining salary. Within the six regions of the United States, average salaries for all respondents ranged from $68,732 in the South Central area to $78,564 in the Northeast region. Fundraisers working for scientific or research organizations enjoyed the highest average salary of $169,731, followed by those individuals employed by consulting agencies ($87,571) and trade/professional associations ($80,051).

Within the three regions of Canada, average salaries for all respondents ranged from C$51,807 in the Eastern provinces area to C$79,245 in the

Central provinces. Fundraisers working for consulting agencies enjoyed the highest average salary of C$89,296, followed by those individuals employed by religion-related organizations (C$80,905) and health services (C$79,538).

Correlation with Certification

The possession of a certification credential correlated positively with salary. Fundraisers in the U.S. possessing the Certified Fund Raising Executive (CFRE) credential earned, on average, $19,000 more than respondents with no certification, while individuals in Canada holding the credential earned C$14,000 more than those who did not. Those individuals possessing the Advanced Certified Fund Raising Executive (ACFRE) credential earned $48,000 more in the U.S. and C$2,400 more in Canada.

As expected, there were also positive correlations between average compensation and the size of an organization's staff, its budget and amount of funds raised, as well as years of professional experience.

Gender Gap

A significant gap continues to exist between the salaries of male and female fundraisers in the United States. Male fundraisers in the United States reported an average salary of $88,071 in 2007. Women earned $66,646 on average. With the exception of 2005 when the salary gap diminished slightly, in the United States the gap has consistently been approximately $20,000 during the eight years in which the survey has been conducted.

The gap in salaries by gender seems to be closing in Canada, where male fundraisers reported an average salary of C$76,980 in 2007 and women earned C$73,627 on average. Seventy-three percent of all survey respondents classified themselves as female, while 25 percent classified themselves as male.

Asked whether they looked for a job with another employer in the last twelve months, 9 percent of United States respondents and 12 percent of Canadian respondents said yes. Top reasons for job leaving were to earn a higher salary; frustration with the work environment; to engage in more interesting or challenging work; opportunities for career advancement elsewhere; unrealistic work expectations; and lack of recognition for one's work.

The survey also addressed health, retirement and other benefits.

2009 Study Highlights

The 2009 AFP Compensation and Benefits Study was undertaken in January 2009. Survey forms were successfully emailed to 21,574 AFP members in the United States and 2,673 AFP members in Canada. A total of 2,966 members completed and returned survey forms by the cut-off date, for an overall response rate of 12 percent.

Demographics

The characteristics of the respondent population mirrored those of the AFP membership at-large.

• Membership statistics at the time of the survey show that approximately 67 percent of AFP members who report their gender in the membership database are female and 24 percent are male. Survey respondents mirrored gender proportionality: females 75 percent, males 24 percent.

• Less than 6 percent of AFP members are non-white. Thirty-seven percent do not report ethnic background. Of the 2,966 survey respondents, 2,962 answered the question on ethnicity. Of these, 90 percent indicated they are Caucasian.

• The types of organizations most represented in AFP membership at the time of the survey are: Educational, Human Services and Health.

Affiliation with these same three organizational types was reported by 61 percent of survey respondents.

• Anecdotal evidence indicates that AFP membership is weighted toward older practitioners. Of the 50 percent of members who report their age range, 72 percent are 40 years of age or older. This was reflected in the survey respondents, with 51 percent reporting they are 45 or older and an additional 26 percent reporting they are between the ages of 35 and 44. The number of practitioners in the 25-34 age range was 21 percent.

About the Survey

Members can download the full report in the "Members Only" section of the AFP website (login is required). Nonmembers may purchase the report for $85 through the AFP Professional Advancement Department at profadv@afpnet.org.

In addition, members and nonmembers may purchase individualized salary reports that allow comparison of your salary to that of individuals whose positions/organizations are comparable to your current or desired position/organization. For more information or to request individualized reports, please contact the AFP Professional Advancement Department at profadv@afpnet.org.

Appendix D

Psychology of Philanthropy – Why People Give

Donors give for the following reasons:

1. Moral obligation to help.

2. Personal satisfaction of helping others.

3. To remove guilt for not giving.

4. To maintain or improve social status, prestige, respect, or acclaim.

5. In response to peer pressure.

6. Out of compassion or empathy.

7. Personal identification with cause or benefactor.

8. Self-interest.

9. Religious influence.

10. The need to be needed.

11. Substitution for active participation in good works.

12. Support for the mission and purpose of the organization.

13. Personal relationship with the organization.

14. Appreciation for the organization's mission.

15. To feel the "glow of emotional virtue."

16. As evidence of one's success and ability to give.

17. To express anger.

18. To express love.

19. To express hope (for a cure)

20. To end fear (of fire, sickness, hell, etc).

21. Out of the cause's appeal (cause célèbre).

22. To be remembered.

23. To gain recognition or attention

24. To join a worthwhile group, sense of belonging.

25. To preserve the species.

26. To gain immortality.

27. For psychic self-satisfaction.

28. For vicarious self-actualization.

29. Giving to oneself (benefactor seen as an extension of one's self).

30. Desire to provide public goods one may use themselves.

31. Desire to provide public goods used by others.

32. Desire to provide public goods so others do not try to use one's own goods.

33. Satisfaction derived from the goods themselves.

34. Satisfaction derived for bringing about the result.

35. To fulfill a condition for employment.

36. In response to leadership from respected peers.

37. Desire to be an agent for "public good."

38. Satisfaction received from seeing others satisfied.

39. Tax benefits.

Appendix E

Suggested Reading

Bolman, Lee G. & Deal, Terrence E.: *Leading with Soul*, Jossey-Bass, San Francisco 1995

Covey, Stephen R.: The 7 *Habits of Highly Effective People,* Simon & Schuster, New York 1989

Panas, Jerold: *Born to Raise,* Pluribus Press, Chicago 1988

Schon, Donald A: *The Reflective Practitioner,* Basic Books, United States 1993

Wagner, Lilya: *Careers in Fundraising,* John Wiley & Sons, New York 2002

Wagner, Lilya & Ryan, J. Patrick (editors): *Fundraising as a Profession,* John Wiley & Sons, New York 2004

Appendix F

Where to Start Looking for a Job as a Professional Fundraiser

Nonprofit Job Guide

In addition to seeking jobs in your local community and through your own networks, there are several other avenues available to you. The first one is to seek the services of a professional executive search firm, or headhunter. If you choose to go this route, you should look for a firm that specializes in the nonprofit field, because it will have a much better understanding of what you are looking for and will be more knowledgeable about careers that are available in fundraising. Also there are numerous online job services for nonprofit. Here are a few of my favorites.

My Top 15

Association of Fundraising Professionals
The AFP has 30,000 members in 206 chapters across the globe. Its nonprofit job board boasts over 200 nonprofit positions available nationally. Users can also access career resources via the website to assist in landing a job. Many local chapters have their own regional job boards as well. www.afpnet.org

CharityChannel
Founded in 1992, CharityChannel has over 100,000 participants. It is a nonprofit networking organization and its job listing board lists available vacancies in the nonprofit sector around the country. Job seekers can organize their search by country, position, job title or employer. www.charitychannel.com

CharityVillage
With over 3,500 pages of jobs and career resources, CharityVillage is Canada's premiere site for accessing positions in the nonprofit sector. It is easily navigable and allows the user to filter their search by location and keyword. www.charityvillage.com/applicants/jobs.asp

Chronicle of Philanthropy
The *Chronicle of Philanthropy* is the largest publication for the field of philanthropy. The *Chronicle* has hard copy and online job listings as well as good information about the nonprofit sector and fundraising. www.philanthropy.com/sections/jobs

idealist.org
A subsidiary group of Action Without Borders, a nonprofit organization founded in 1995, the stated goal of idealist.org is to network people, associations and resources to create a better tomorrow. The site includes a list of career opportunities available to the user, including over 4,000 jobs and 16,000 volunteer positions. www.idealist.org

NYTimes & Monster: Nonprofit Jobs
The *New York Times* teamed up with Monster, the largest job board on the Net, to create a comprehensive nonprofit job board. This board boasts more than 1,000 jobs posted each month all over the country. You search by job posting date, career level, years of experience, or education level. www.jobmarket.nytimes.com

Independent Sector
Independent Sector is a leadership forum to facilitate the advancement of the common good, both nationally and internationally. It has vacancies listed primarily from organizations from the Washington DC metropolitan area. www.independentsector.org

National Council of Nonprofits
The National Council of Nonprofits lists nonprofit job openings from around the country. Users can upload resumes and search by keyword, location and job type. www.councilofnonprofits.org

OpportunityKnocks.org
Opportunity Knocks is a nationally-oriented website that caters specifically to nonprofit opportunities. It provides a range of filters to assist job-seekers in narrowing down their preferences between geography, field and employment type. Furthermore, the site lets employers search for possible employees and gather information that can improve and support their organization. www.opportunityknocks.org

Philanthropy Journal
The *Philanthropy Journal's* nonprofit job search site not only allows applicants to sort jobs by category, field of interest and state, but also provides a comprehensive listing of resources to assist nonprofit workers. In addition, it posts news bulletins to inform users about current events in the nonprofit job market. www.philanthropyjournal.org

Philanthropy News Digest
Philanthropy News Digest lists nonprofit jobs available across the country. It provides career resources including articles and notifications of upcoming events. Job seekers can filter their search by organization type, job function and state. www.foundationcenter.org/pnd

The NonProfit Times
The NonProfit Times is a business publication for nonprofit management. Users can register to use the site and access its nonprofit job listings. There are also articles and links to career resources pertaining to the nonprofit sector. www.nptimes.com/career.html

ThirdSectorJobs
ThirdSectorJobs currently has over 400 positions listed for charity jobs, voluntary work and nonprofit charities. Users can search by keyword, upload their resumes and create a job seeker profile. The site also provides career advice. www.thirdsector.co.uk

Yahoo! hotjobs

Yahoo's nonprofit job board automatically provides a listing of openings in the user's area. It also suggests websites that might help in acquiring that coveted nonprofit position. Job seekers can narrow their choices based on keywords, location and category. www.hotjobs.yahoo.com

The above list has been adapted from a list of 100 job listing sites prepared by Nathan Grimm, SR Education Group. The complete list can be accessed at www.reachnetwork.com.

Appendix G

Glossary

Advanced Certified Fund Raising Executive (ACFRE): a credential earned by an individual who meets specific requirements including previous certification (see Certified Fund Raising Executive). This credentialing process was developed and is administered by the Association of Fundraising Professionals.

Annual giving: a fundraising program that generates gift support on an annual basis.

Association of Fundraising Professionals (AFP): a professional society (headquartered in Arlington, Virginia) that fosters the development and growth of fundraising professionals, works to advance philanthropy and volunteerism and promotes high ethical standards in the fundraising profession. (Formerly the National Society of Fundraising Executives.)

Capital campaign: an intensive fundraising effort to meet a specific financial goal within a specified period of time for one or more major projects that are out of the ordinary, such as the construction of a facility, the purchase of equipment, or the acquisition of endowment funds.

Case: the reasons why an organization both needs and merits philanthropic support, usually by outlining the organization's programs, current needs and plans.

Certified Fund Raising Executive (CFRE): a designation conferred by Certified Fund Raising Executive International that is awarded to a professional fundraiser who has met specified standards of service, experience and knowledge.

Charitable deduction: the portion of a gift to a qualified charity that is deductible from an individual's or a corporation's federal income tax, an individual's gift tax, or an individual's estate tax.

Charitable foundation: a corporation or trust set up and operated exclusively for charitable purposes. It might be established for the support of a particular charity, or it might make grants to multiple charities.

Chief development officer (CDO): the highest-ranking development staff member responsible for a development program.

Chief executive officer (CEO): the highest-ranking executive responsible for organizational operations.

Chief financial officer (CFO): a senior staff member responsible for the financial management of an organization, including budget control, cash-flow management, financial forecasting and related functions.

Development: the total process by which an organization increases public understanding of its mission and acquires financial support for its programs.

Development office: the department or division of an organization responsible for all facets of its development program.

Director of development (DOD): an individual who manages the development programs of an organization

Donor Bill of Rights: the statement of rights provided a donor. (See Appendix B.)

Executive director: an individual who manages or directs an organization's affairs. It is the organization's chief executive officer.

501(c)(3): the section of the Internal Revenue Code that exempts certain types of organizations (such as charitable, religious, scientific, literary, and educational) from federal taxation and permits these organizations to receive tax deductible donations. For information about other 501(c) organizations, see the IRS Tax Code.

Fundraiser: an individual, paid or volunteer, who plans, manages, or participates in raising assets and resources for an organization or cause.

Fundraising: the raising of assets and resources from various sources for the support of an organization or a specific project.

Independent sector: nonprofit or tax-exempt organizations collectively that are specifically not associated with any government, government agency, or commercial enterprise.

Major gift: a significant donation to a nonprofit organization, the amount required to qualify as a major gift being determined by the organization.

Mission statement: a statement about a societal need or value that an organization proposes to address.

Philanthropy: love of humankind, usually expressed by an effort to enhance the well-being of humanity through personal acts of practical kindness or by financial support of a cause or causes, such as a charity, mutual aid or assistance (service clubs, youth groups), quality of life (arts, education, environment) and religion.

Private inurement: the receiving (such as by a board member, staff member, stockholder, or business owner) of financial benefit of the net profits from an endeavor. Nonprofit organizations cannot legally provide private inurement to any entity.

Pro bono: commonly used to designate work done without charge by a professional.

Prospect research: the continuing search for pertinent information on prospects and donors.

Special event: a function designed to attract and involve people in an organization or cause.

Stakeholder: a person (such as a volunteer, client, donor, or employee) who has a special interest in the activities and decisions of an organization.

Stewardship: a process whereby an organization seeks to be worthy of continued philanthropic support, including the acknowledgment of gifts, donor recognition, the honoring of donor intent, prudent investment of gifts and the effective and efficient use of funds to further the mission of the organization.

Strategic plan: decisions and actions that shape and guide an organization while emphasizing the future implications of present decisions. This plan usually employs the SWOT analysis.

SWOT analysis (strengths, weaknesses, opportunities, threats): an integral component of a planning process that examines an organization's internal strengths and weaknesses and the external opportunities and threats that will impact its program in the market or markets in which it operates.

Vision statement: a statement about what an organization can and should become at some future time.

Adapted from the Association of Fundraising Professionals (AFP) Dictionary of Fundraising Terms

Index

CPSIA information can be obtained at www.ICGtesting.com
Printed in the USA
LVOW071201251112

308660LV00003B/425/P